Table of

Introduction

Deciding to Raise Chicken.

Choosing the Best Chicken Breeds

Raising Chicks

Raising Juvenile Chickens

Starting with Adult Birds

Chicken Coops

Eggs!

Incubating and Hatching Chicks

Parasites and Disease

Conclusion

Work Cited

Introduction

First, I want to thank you and congratulate you for downloading, "Raising Chickens: Backyard Chickens for Beginners: Choosing the Best Breed, Feeding and Care, and Raising Chickens for Eggs."

This book contains all of the basic strategies and proven practices for anyone ready to start their own backyard chicken flock! My hope is that this book gives you the confidence you need to begin raising chickens and ultimately enjoy fresh eggs and the satisfaction that comes with living a self-sustaining lifestyle. If you will apply the concepts and practices within this book, I can promise that you will truly enjoy raising your chickens. Here's to fresh eggs and living the chicken life!

Deciding to Raise Chickens

Do you ever think that you would like to raise chickens but you just don't know where to start? Perhaps you want to eat healthier and would love fresh eggs and meat but you don't know anything about raising chickens. Maybe you've even considered some of these questions: Do I need a rooster for eggs? What will I do with the extra eggs? What if I live in the city? Can I justify the added expense of raising chickens? Luckily for you, the versatility of raising chickens makes all of these scenarios possible for anyone! In short, chickens are hardy, and with a little feed, shelter, and care, you can go from not knowing anything about raising chickens to being an "expert in all things chicken" in a very short amount of time. And by the way, you actually don't need a rooster for egg production, which means a small backyard coop can go completely unnoticed by your neighbors. Finally, don't worry about producing too many eggs. You can always sell your extra eggs (and even meat) to cover the costs of feeding and caring for you chickens. Believe it or not, fresh (organic) eggs are very desirable to those individuals seeking to lead a healthy lifestyle. Maybe you'll even make a profit!

Like with any well thought out project, a little research goes a long way. It is amazing how emotionally invested you may become with your chickens, so before you invest time, sweat, and especially your hard earned dollars into keeping a few chickens, be sure to review this entire book so that you are equipped with the knowledge you need to successfully raise your chickens (Foley, 2015). Once you're equipped with this information, you'll have to decide whether you're going to start with chicks or adults. For purposes of this book, we'll start with chicks. If you should decide to start with adults, you may want to skip to the **Starting with Adult Birds** chapter.

Choosing the Best Chicken Breeds

There are an estimated 19 billion chickens in the world according to statistics from the Food and Agriculture Organization of the United Nations, (Food and Agriculuture Organization of the United States Statistics Division, 2013), so choosing your chicken breed(s) may seem like a daunting task. But, to make it easier on you, let's talk about some of the most popular breeds (in the U.S.) and some of the tips to help narrow down the choices.

First, start with where you live and ask yourself how you plan to house your birds. Certain breeds are more equipped to handle colder climates versus hotter climates, and vice versa. Some birds handle confinement well while other breeds prefer room to roam. Temperament is also a valid consideration, where some breeds are calm and others are flighty.

The next question to ask yourself: Do you want chickens for meat, eggs, both, or just because they're pretty to look at? Lucky for you, there are breeds that fall into each category! Some of the top meat breeds include the Cornish Cross, Jersey Giant, Bresse, Freedom Rangers and Orpington. (Morning Chores, n.d.) The Orpington is also one of the top egg-laying breeds. Additionally, some of the most popular egg-laying breeds include the Rhode Island Red, Leghorn, Black Star, and Ameraucana. (Backyard Chicken Farmer, n.d.) Breeds that are good for both meat and eggs, such as the Orpington, are known as "dual purpose." Dual purpose chcikens include the Brown Leghorn, Egyptian Fayoumi, Turken, Buckeye, and Chantecler. (Morning Chores, n.d.) For those who care more about how the chicken looks than what they're used for, there are several "ornamental" chicken breeds that look pretty, while at the same time,produce some eggs and/or meat. The ornamental birds include the Cochin; known for its extremely fluffy looking appearance, the Polish; known for it's "top hat," and the Phoenix chicken; known for it's long tail which can reach between two to five feet in length! (Stromberg's Chicks & Game Birds Unlimited, n.d.)

While oftentimes a mixed breed chicken may be the answer, those wishing to take on purebreds can view a list of heritage chicken breeds at https://livestockconservancy.org/images/uploads/docs/pick achicken.pdf. According to the site, a heritage chicken must adhere to the APA breed standards, be capable of naturally mating, have a long, productive outdoor lifespan, and have a slow growth rate. (The Livestock Conservancy, n.d.) Still not sure what to get? Your local feed store with chicks for sale will usually be glad to help you. Additionally, all of the major hatcheries have a direct dial phone number for any questions you may have regarding selecting the right breed for you.

Raising Chicks

Generally, chicks are bought in store, at a farm, or even online when they are only a few days old. One of the benefits to the chicks being so small at this stage is that the setup you will need to sustain them for the first four weeks of their lives is also small. The container you use to house the chicks (whatever you decide to use), is known as the "brooder". The brooder can be made from several different containers- i.e., a kiddie pool, a plastic storage tub, a wooden box, etc. While the chicks don't have to be kept indoors, like most babies, they do need to be kept warm, so a housing area that is draft and harsh weather-free as well as predator proof is essential. Be sure not to close the chicks up too tight, because ventilation is a key to their survival. If you don't want to have to constantly upgrade the chick's brooder, the rule of thumb is to allow two square feet per chick. At first, this may seem like a large space compared to the chicks' size, but as they grow you'll see why this is ideal. If you do decide to keep them indoors, be aware that baby chicks like to "scratch" their bedding materials. This is an instinct that carries over into adulthood and helps the chicks to find food in the soil and grass. However, when scratching while indoors, this creates a very fine dust that settles everywhere within the room they are in. The bigger the chicks become, the more dust they create. This is something to consider if planning to keep the chicks indoors and especially if planning to keep a large number of chicks. (The My Pet Chicken Guide to Chicken Care, n.d.)

Heat is essential to a baby chick's survival. Since they don't have their mothers to provide warmth, a proper substitute is necessary. Red-bulb heat lamps are the standard for providing heat to baby chicks (White bulbs are an option but have been known to cause the chicks to pick at one another). The chicks need to be kept at 90-95 degrees Fahrenheit for the first week of their lives. Each week after that you can reduce the temperature by 5 degrees per week until you reach 70 degrees. By this point, their "fluff" will be turning into feathers and they can self-regulate their own body temperatures and will not need artificial heat. While heat lamps are often the first choice for providing warmth to baby chicks, they can also be dangerous and are notorious for causing fires. Hang the light no closer than 18 inches from the floor, and do not allow it to touch any substances that may melt or catch on fire. It's okay if the area directly beneath the heat lamp is higher than 90 degrees Fahrenheit as long as the chicks have room to move away from the heat as well. Chicks that are content with the temperature in their brooder will be evenly dispersed throughout the container. If the chicks are too cold, they will all huddle directly under the heat source. If the chicks are too hot, they will move as far away from the heat source as possible. Open-mouth breathing is a sign of extreme heat distress and needs to be addressed quickly or the chicks may die.

Equally as important as a warm dry enclosure, is food and water for your new arrivals. A one-gallon "waterer" for every 50 chicks you have should be sufficient initially. If chicks are not eating and drinking soon after arriving, you may need to help them dip their beaks in the water to teach them where the water source is. Be careful not to submerge the nostrils, just the tips of the beaks! Also, many people place marbles in the "waterers" during the chicks first week. The colorful marbles attract the chicks to the lifesaving water but also take up room within the dish so the chicks can only get their beaks in so far, which ideally helps prevent drowning. Giving the chicks hydration and nutrients is especially important for chicks that have been shipped to you. During the hatching process, chicks absorb the majority of the yolk, which has been nourishing them while they develop inside the egg. This absorption can sustain the chick for 2-3 days after hatching, even without any other food or water being provided. With a mother hen, the chicks usually stay under the hen for this time period to dry out from hatching and to allow some of the later eggs in the nest to hatch. However, since shipping from a hatchery to your doorstep usually takes up to 2-3 days, the chicks will be hungry and thirsty when they first arrive at your home.

Commercial chick starters are the ideal feed for the first eight weeks of your chicks' lives. These feeds are a crumble and generally contain about 20 percent protein. Different stages of feed are available in mash, crumble, and pellet forms, all of which describe the size of the feed. Mash is the smallest, then crumble, and then pellets. (Mormino, n.d.) This is the highest percentage of protein chicks will ever need to consume throughout their lifetime. This makes sense considering the chicks' extreme growth rate in the first few months of their lives. There are many different feed brands to choose from, including options for medicated or non-medicated feed. Deciding on a particular feed usually boils down to personal preference. Some people prefer medicated feed because it gives the chicks' immune systems a boost (especially since they are in a brooder as opposed to outside on the ground where they would naturally receive immunities from pecking through the dirt). The "boost" comes from the amprolium, which is usually found in medicated feed, and protects chicks against coccidiosis, which is a common and often deadly intestinal disease that is spread by fecal matter. *If your chicks have received the coccidiosis vaccine or you plan on giving it, DO NOT feed the chicks medicated starter feed, as it will render the vaccine useless and make the chicks vulnerable to disease.*

When purchasing chicks from a hatchery, they often offer vaccinations at an additional price per chick. The above is a prime example of why it is important to know which vaccines your chicks have received. (Mormino, n.d.) Others prefer non-medicated options with the thought that medication should only be used if a problem arises. Chicks should have feed available to them at all times and the feeders should be adequately sized so that the chicks do not appear to be trampling over each other to get to the feed. Trial and error will help determine the best route for your chicks, but regardless of which route you choose, make sure to keep your chicks in a clean, dry environment. Overcrowding, excess filth, and wet and warm (from the necessary heat source) conditions cause coccidiosis and other potentially deadly microorganisms to thrive.

Starter feeds have been researched and commercially produced to provide your chicks with 100 percent of their necessary dietary requirements. However, as your chicks grow, should you decide to give them treats, grains or other fibrous foods, they will require grit to help digest them. Grit is any hard material such as sand, dirt, or small stones that aid in digestion. If outside with the mother hen, the chicks would naturally pick these things up while foraging for food. If chicks are inside or kept enclosed with no access to the ground, grit must be supplied to them (Mormino, n.d.)

Chick mortality is natural and some deaths usually occur even if it is the mother hen that is raising the chicks. However, a hard shipping trip can increase the number of chicks that die or look poorly upon arrival to your home. If this appears to be the case, some additional steps can be taken to help increase your chicks' chances. In addition to the standard feed and water suggestions mentioned previously, you can put six tablespoons of sugar in each gallon of water provided for the chicks. You can also try mixing some of the extra sweet water with some of the feed to make a gruel-like mix. After three or four days of this special feed and water mix, you should see improvement, and the chicks should be over the stress of shipping.

Another sign to watch for in the chicks that is often caused by shipping stress, is something commonly referred to as "pasty butt." This is manure that has become stuck to the back end of the chick. This blockage needs to be removed daily. The easiest way to remove the manure is by holding the chick's backside under warm water and gently removing the manure with a soft cloth. Make sure to dry the chick sufficiently so that it does not get chilled upon returning to the brooder. If the "pasty butt" does not clear up after a few days, you may have a more serious problem such as coccidiosis, which will require medication to treat. (Murray McMurray Hatchery, n.d.)

Raising Juvenile Chickens

You will have about four weeks from the time your newly hatched chicks arrive until they are feathered out enough (and pooping enough!) to go outside of the brooder and into their permanent coop. Ideally, you should have your coop built or purchased before you chicks even arrive because those four weeks will go fast! Even if you plan to free range your chickens, they will need a "coop" of sorts to go into at night, especially in the case of inclement weather. If you're afraid of your chickens getting lost or falling prey to predators, a happy compromise may be a coop with a run attached to it, or a moveable version of a coop known as a "chicken tractor". A "chicken tractor" has an area that allows the chickens access to the grass while still keeping them fully enclosed and safe. The tractors only vary in that they are usually on wheels and can be moved from place to place to allow the chickens access to fresh grass as often as you are willing to move them. Inside the chicken coop, regardless of what design you go with, you should allow 2-3 square feet per chicken, and in the outside run, you should have enough room for 8-10 square feet per chicken. Of course, if you decide to free range, the run requirements won't apply. Rather, you should use a rule of thumb of 250 to 300 free range square feet per bird.

Do not skimp on the space requirements for your flock as this can cause stress, cannibalism, pecking, and sometimes even death. While it may seem like too much room when your four-week-old chicks first venture outside, as they grow, you will be glad you built or purchased accommodations that will comfortably house your flock when they become adult birds. Obviously, you may be able to get away with less space per bird if your birds are a smaller breed (such as Bantams),.But you may need more space if your birds are one of the large fowl breeds. Use your judgment and allow your chickens as large of a coop as you can financially and spatially afford. Raising and caring for chickens can be an addicting hobby, and just because you only have ten chicks now, doesn't mean you'll only have ten chicks this time next year! (For Dummies, n.d.)

Chickens are creatures of habit, and they are also prey animals. As adults, every night around dusk your chickens will "put themselves up" into their coop and come out again when the sun rises. Normally, chicks would be taught this by the mother hen, but if you are raising the chicks yourself, a little encouragement from you will probably be necessary to show them where they should go. This is especially important if you are free ranging your chicks. Chicks who aren't closed up in a coop will almost definitely become susceptible prey to nighttime predators or the natural elements.

At about eight weeks of age, you can transition your chicks from chick starter feed to chick starter/grower feed.

The grower feed will have slightly reduced protein content than regular starter feed (approximately 18% protein). Continue to provide grit to your chicks if they have not been moved onto the ground, but ideally, by now they have been, or else you may have some pretty unhappy chickens!

At 18 weeks, your "chicks" are now more appropriately known as pullets and cockerels. A pullet is a young hen that is less than a year old and a cockerel is a young male chicken. (Merriam-Webster, n.d.) The cockerels will be well on their way to crowing (if they aren't already), and your pullets are preparing for egg-laying (assuming they are a breed that begins to do so at approximately six months of age, which is usually the case).

The last and final "level" of feed is layer feed. This feed contains calcium (to help with healthy egg production), but it can also permanently damage the kidneys, cause kidney stones, reduce lifetime egg production, and shorten a bird's lifespan if fed to chickens younger than 18 weeks. However, if your chickens have begun egg-laying already, it is not only acceptable to give them layer feed, but recommended.

Calcium, as previously mentioned, is an important part of healthy egg production. Your hens layer feed contains some calcium, but it doesn't hurt to provide them with a supplemental supply in the form of crushed oyster shell. Make it available to your birds in a separate dish from their regular feed, so that each hen can decide for herself how much extra to take into her body. All laying hens have different calcium requirements, and forcing them to consume supplemental calcium with their regular feed may lead to the opposite problem, too much calcium.

Lastly in relation to feed, and perhaps most important, is the fact that chicken "scratch" is *not* meant to be chickens sole source of feed. While it is often made of various things, scratch consists primarily of cracked corn, wheat, oats, sunflower seeds, millet and various other seeds.. It is a source of energy, but not a good source of vitamins, minerals or protein. Therefore, scratch should be fed sparingly, if at all. (Damerow, 2012) If you do choose to give scratch, give it in cold weather, just before dusk, as it is a decent source of energy at that time of year. Once again, give it sparingly, not as a sole feed source, as too much of it can lead to obesity and even death. Just like when they were chicks, birds on layer feed should be free fed. This insures that all members of the flock are getting the full nutritional amounts that they need. (Mormino, n.d.)

Starting with Adult Birds

Some people may wish to skip the entire "raising chicks" process and begin immediately with adult birds. This may save you some hassle in terms of housing and protecting babies but it will cost you in terms of initial purchase price. While chicks can be obtained year round for some breeds and may only cost a few dollars apiece, adult hens will more likely be somewhere around twenty dollars each and will be in high demand in spring time when everyone else has the same idea as you, a homegrown omelet! Adult roosters are usually easy to find any time of the year and are relatively cheap, if not free. This is because you only need one rooster per 10 hens for good fertility and you don't need ANY roosters if you are solely interested in eggs, not producing chicks. Therefore, roosters of all ages are usually readily available. It is possible to keep multiple roosters, especially within a large flock, but watch out for extreme bullying or over-mating.

All flocks will develop a pecking order but overcrowding with too many roosters to hens will cause problems. Your flock's dominant roo will be easily identifiable after a few days of careful observation. If new birds are being added to a flock, or your flock is coming into breeding age, the competing birds will work out the pecking order by having a "face-off". During the face-off, two roos will face each other and raise their hackles (one of the long narrow feathers on the neck or saddle of a bird (Hackle, n.d.)), and attack each other with their feet. The winner is generally the dominant roo. The winning roo will get first dibs on mating with hens and available food. Be careful to keep an eye out for lower birds on the totem pole. Excessive fighting can lead to starvation and gnarly wounds. Over-mating can also occur when there are too may roos for the number of hens available. This can lead to the hens being injured from over mating. The tell-tale signs of over-mating include severe feather loss on the hens' backs, wings, or the back of their heads. When mating, the rooster holds onto the hen with his feet digging into her back and his beak holding the back of her head, and, these are often the areas you will notice feather loss. Once the feathers are gone, continued mating can sometimes lead to the roos puncturing the hen's skin while mating. If you don't notice this in time, or just want to protect your hens before this feather loss occurs, chicken saddles are a major trend right now. Chicken saddles are apron-like saddles made out of material that help protect the hen from feather loss, or allow lost feathers time to grow back and back wounds time to heal. (Chicken Help Q: Is it possible for several roosters to coexist peacefully together in our flock?, n.d.) Repeated fights or over-mating may require you to find a new home for one or several of your roos.

When looking for a hen that is already producing eggs but not "worn out" in terms of her laying life, choose a hen that is already 6 months of age. If the chicken(s) you are considering purchasing are on the verge of egg laying, these are some of the signs to look for, which will help you determine if she is already laying. Comb, wattle and leg color are an easy-to-spot sign. The comb on a chicken is easy to remember as it is similar to where a comb would be used on a person's head. The chicken's comb is the soft part on top of its head. Both males and females have them, however, they are larger on the male than the female. While some breeds have variations, almost all combs are red in color.

Chickens' combs come in several different varieties: buttercup, cushion, pea, rose, silkis, single, strawberry, and v-shaped. Comb-type is irrelevant to some backyard chicken keepers and at the same time very necessary to others (it can help determine a chicken's breed for those looking to own only purebreds or to present their chickens for show). Combs that appear "pointy" are what we generally envision when we picture the standard chicken, including the buttercup, single, and rose combs. The "buttercup" comb has a single leader from the base of the beak to a cup-shaped crown that is set firmly on the center of the skull and entirely surmounted by a circle of regular points. The "single comb" is a mostly thin, fleshy formation of smooth soft surface texture, firmly attached from the beak along the top of the skull with a strong base. The top portion shows five or six rather deep serrations or distinct points, the middle points being higher than the anterior or posterior, forming a semi-oval when viewed from the side. It is divided into three sections; the front or anterior, the middle, extending past the rear base of the skull, and the posterior or blade. The "rose," unlike the buttercup and single combs, is a solid, nearly flat on top (although it should be slightly convex and studded with small rounded protuberances), comb-lacking points other than the low, fleshly one that terminates in a well-developed tapering spike at its tip. The "cushion comb" is also a solid, low, moderately small comb, which is smooth on top. Its front, rear, and sides are nearly straight with rounded corners and it has no spikes, giving it the appearance of a pea (hence its name). Also named due to its appearance, the "strawberry" is a low comb but it is set forward on the face of a chicken. Its shape and surface resemble the outer part of half a strawberry with a large end nearest the beak of the chicken.

A third easily identifiable comb is the "v-shaped" comb. It is formed of two well-defined horn sections that are joined at their base. This type of comb is seen on Houdans, Polish, Crevecoueurs, LeFleche, and Sultan chickens. The "walnut" comb also looks almost exactly like its namesake. It is big, pitted, round, and can grow shockingly to almost the size of and cover the chicken's face! (The 9 Comb Types, 2015) The "silikis" comb gives its breeds an almost regal appearance. It is an almost round, somewhat lumpy comb, generally greater in width than length, and covered with small corrugations on top and crossed with narrow transverse indentation slightly to the front of the comb. Sometimes there are two or three small rear points hidden by a crest, but not always. (Combs, n.d.) The Standard of Perfection often has very specific descriptions in regard to what a purebred chicken's comb should resemble, and those that do not are often disqualified in the show ring. But don't confuse a chicken's comb with its wattle. While the chicken's comb rests on top of its head, its wattle is the fleshy pendulous process that lies underneath its beak. (Wattle, n.d.)

Now that you know what the chicken's comb and wattles are, you can use their color as a good indication of a hen that is laying. A hen that is a good layer will have waxy red combs and wattles, paler or "bleached" legs, and large moist vents wide enough to allow eggs to pass through (three fingers wide between the pelvic bones). The "vent" of a chicken is the workhorse of the chicken. The vent does it all: poops, pees, and lays eggs. It all comes out of the same place. In order to investigate your chicken's vent, you will have to get up close and friendly. Flip your chicken over and expose her underside, but be careful not to suffocate her. The vent or cloaca is located underneath the tail where the digestive waste to comes out. Interestingly enough, when it comes to chickens, the vent is where EVERYTHING comes out, and goes in; meaning this is where the rooster fertilizes the hen, the egg comes out AND where the waste comes out. Chickens don't have a bladder and therefore don't urinate. Rather, the urinary system waste, also known as urates, are simply dumped in with the digestive wastes at the end of the digestive system. That's why chicken droppings appear to contain white urates mixed with darker digested material. (Gautheir & Ludlow, n.d.) Bet you'll never think of a chicken egg the same ever again!

Once your hens begin laying regularly, she will lay one egg per 24 hours on average. If your chickens are free ranging, encourage your hens to lay where you want by providing a dark/private nest box perhaps with some bedding and maybe even with a fake egg or two. Chickens are habitual and visual when it comes to egg laying. Once your hen finds the place she likes to lay, she will lay an egg there every day until she has enough to sit on. If this is not the place you want her to lay, discourage her from using the site as a nest by removing the egg daily, making the area less private, blocking her access to it. If you are getting several eggs each day in the same spot, this means several hens are sharing this nest and you might as well let them continue to lay there (assuming the spot is protected from predators and the elements). Remember that lots of things affect egg production, so it is not especially worrisome if your hens skip a day here or there. Breed, temperature, weather, and several other factors can determine how many eggs a hen will lay in any given year.

Some hens produce many eggs but have no desire to sit on them and hatch them out. Other breeds lay very few eggs but love to hatch and mother their chicks. This act is known as "going broody." A broody hen is one that has stopped laying eggs and is now trying to hatch out chicks, she may even sit on other hen's eggs if she doesn't have any eggs of her own. Some hens will lay for approximately 2-3 weeks straight and then will go broody. A broody hen will often be very protective of her nest (regardless of whether or not she has any eggs in there). She may not come off of the nest even to eat or drink, and may ruffle her feathers and growl when you, another chicken, or a predator tries to remove her or her eggs from the nest. Overtime, you will learn the temperaments of your birds and how hard or easy it will be to collect eggs from a broody hen. If you are raising chickens solely for their eggs, it's best to collect the eggs daily to ensure that the hen hasn't had time to start incubating the egg (causing the embryo to begin developing). General grocery store eggs are not fertile, therefore, if you have a partially developed egg, there is no chance of cracking open a developing egg into your morning omelet.

Home-grown eggs that come from a flock that contains a rooster is another story completely. If you find a nest of several eggs that could potentially be several days or over a week old, you might want to consider cracking them into a separate bowl instead of directly into your skillet. This way, if they are developing (or rotten), the rest of your eggs will not be spoiled. Now that you know what channel the egg passes through in the chicken's body to get to your plate, you will realize why some eggs may have dried manure or dirt on them no matter how quickly you collect them out of the nest. The verdict on whether or not to wash eggs is highly debatable. This is because egg-shells are porous, and they have a micro membrane coating on them called a "bloom". The blooms purpose is to keep potential baby chicks and their environment safe and clean. Due to the natural bloom, bacteria have a hard time getting inside a dry eggshell. However, washing dirty eggs removes the bloom and allows bacteria inside the egg. Also, washing dirty eggs in cool water creates a "vacuum" effect that pulls unwanted bacteria inside the egg even faster. So, the best solution is prevention. In an attempt to prevent your eggs from being "dirty" in the first place, clean your nest boxes often. Obviously, this is not as easy if your chickens are nesting in areas other than the provided nest boxes. This is another reason to encourage them to lay in the designated areas. A constant supply of fresh shavings/bedding helps tremendously with keeping eggs clean once they're initially laid.

Secondly, place your roosting bars *higher* than your nesting boxes. Being a prey animal, chickens prefer to roost in the highest part of the coop as possible. If the only thing they have in their coop to sit on or in is their nesting boxes, they will do so, and they will soil the shavings meant to keep the eggs clean. Building their roosting areas higher than their nesting areas will discourage them from roosting in and soiling their boxes. While these tips will help prevent most of your eggs from getting dirty, it is almost impossible to prevent all of them. While you may choose to allow the dirty eggs to be hatched by your hen, or yourself, being dirty is not a reason to write them off for breakfast. Egg cleaning options include sandpaper-use a fine grit sandpaper to gently sand off any soiled areas of the egg. Even though this damages some of the bloom coating, it helps prevent the "vacuum" effect by keeping the egg dry. If you do choose to use water to clean your eggs, do so with warm/hot water (that is approximately twenty degrees (or more) hotter than the egg itself). Ideally, only wash eggs that are visibly soiled. Anything that comes in that is visibly clean can go straight into the carton. (Winger, n.d.)

Eggs can be kept on the countertop. However, like with any food product, cool temperatures help reduce bacteria growth and extend shelf life so the refrigerator is also an option for storing your eggs, just as you would with grocery store eggs. Eggs that have potentially had some or all of their bloom removed through slight scrubbing or washing should definitely be kept in the refrigerator. You can even place eggs that you intend to incubate later in the refrigerator for up to two weeks with no reduced fertility side effects! Just be sure to place the eggs large end up in the carton.

Chicken Coops

If you started with chicks and have been avoiding deciding what coop to go with, or stringing your chicks along by moving them into bigger and bigger containers, you are now at the point of no return. By six months, your cute fluffy chicks will most likely look like adult chickens and this is because they are! And if you started with adult chickens, you need to decide on a coop right away, unless you plan and raising free-range chickens. With most breeds, your chickens will be capable of breeding and egg-laying at this point and they really need a permanent place to call home. The potential coop designs are endless. And for a small backyard flock of just a few birds, you can most likely get away with purchasing a coop for approximately $300.00 on average. If you are big on do it yourself projects, you can purchase a coop design or imagine it up yourself. The cost of materials and purchasing a design will most likely be roughly the same price, but you may be able to get a much larger coop out of doing it yourself. Your chickens don't care, but nowadays, coops that can be concealed in a city back yard by appearing as mini cottages or blending into the landscape are very popular. It is almost a guarantee that your first coop won't be your last coop. As your flock grows, you become a more experienced chicken keeper and you will inevitably find design flaws or unmet space requirements that you didn't consider when you built your first coop. This is all part of the experience! When choosing your coop, the main things to remember are "per bird spacing," (which was discussed earlier), ventilation, ensuring the coop is predator and weather proof, and if you're planning on collecting eggs, making the nest boxes easily accessible.

Eggs!

On the topic of eggs, without getting too technical, a basic understanding of egg production will help you with your overall management of your mature reproductive flock. Unlike most mammals, hens have only one functional ovary, the left one, situated in the body cavity near the backbone. As a newly hatched chick, your (now grown) hen had up to 4,000 tiny ova or reproductive cells within her body. Throughout the course of her egg laying life, some of the ova will develop into full-sized yolks, each of which is enclosed in a thin-walled sac, or follicle, and attached to the ovary which being supplied richly with blood. When the sac ruptures, the mature yolk is released and it goes into the funnel of the left oviduct. While the right oviduct exists, it is nonfunctional. The left oviduct is coiled and divided into five distinct sections, all totaling approximately 80 cm in length. The egg spends about fifteen minutes in the first section, known as the funnel or infundibulum.

While a hen will lay eggs once reproductively mature regardless of whether or not a rooster is present, if a viable rooster is present and has been breeding with her, this is where fertilization will occur. Section 2 is the Magnun, where the egg will spend about three hours while albumen (the white part of the egg) is secreted and layered around. Section three is the Isthmus, where the egg will spend about one hour while the inner and outer membranes are added, as are some water and mineral salts. Section four is the Shell Gland or uterus, this is where the egg spends the most time during production, roughly twenty-one hours. During this time, some more water is added making the outer white thinner. Then, the shell material (mainly calcium carbonate which is why calcium is so important to egg laying hens) is added. Pigments may also be added to make the shell brown or various other colors depending on your chickens' breed(s). Eggs come in a beautiful array of colors including white, brown, pink, green, and blue. The eggshell color does not affect the nutritional value of the egg.

Lastly, the egg passes through section five of the oviduct, the vagina or cloaca. It passes through this section in less than one minute, and this section has no other known function in the egg's formation. (Jeffrey A. Coutts, 2007) At this point, your hen has laid one of the roughly 4,000 ova that were available to her at hatching, which has matured into what we now call an egg. This is not to say she will lay 4,000 eggs in her lifetime, because not all of the ova will mature. However, once the first egg is laid, many other ova are at various stages of development within the hen. An egg laying hen that is dissected will contain what looks like a string of beads with each bead being slightly larger than the previous, and the largest being an almost fully formed egg.

Now, let's get into the basics of egg-laying and collecting. Once your hens begin laying regularly, she will lay one egg per 24 hours on average. If your chickens are free ranging, encourage your hens to lay where you want by providing a dark and private nest box perhaps with some bedding and maybe even with a fake egg or two. Chickens are habitual and visual when it comes to egg laying. Once your hen finds the place she likes to lay, she will lay an egg there every day until she has enough to sit on. If this is not the place you want her to lay, discourage her from using the site as a nest by removing the egg daily, making the area less private, blocking her access to it. If you are getting several eggs each day in the same spot, this means several hens are sharing this nest and you might as well let them continue to lay there (assuming the spot is protected from predators and the elements). Remember that lots of things affect egg production, so it is not especially worrisome if your hens skip a day here or there. Breed, temperature, weather, and several other factors can determine how many eggs a hen will lay in any given year.

Some hens produce many eggs but have no desire to sit on them and hatch them out. Other breeds lay very few eggs but love to hatch and mother their chicks. This act is known as "going broody." A broody hen is one that has stopped laying eggs and is now trying to hatch out chicks, she may even sit on other hen's eggs if she doesn't have any eggs of her own. Some hens will lay for approximately 2-3 weeks straight and then will go broody. A broody hen will often be very protective of her nest (regardless of whether or not she has any eggs in there). She may not come off of the nest even to eat or drink, and may ruffle her feathers and growl when you, another chicken, or a predator tries to remove her or her eggs from the nest.

Overtime, you will learn the temperaments of your birds and how hard or easy it will be to collect eggs from a broody hen. If you are raising chickens solely for their eggs, it's best to collect the eggs daily to ensure that the hen hasn't had time to start incubating the egg (causing the embryo to begin developing). General grocery store eggs are not fertile, therefore, if you have a partially developed egg, there is no chance of cracking open a developing egg into your morning omelet.

Home-grown eggs that come from a flock that contains a rooster is another story completely. If you find a nest of several eggs that could potentially be several days or over a week old, you might want to consider cracking them into a separate bowl instead of directly into your skillet. This way, if they are developing (or rotten), the rest of your eggs will not be spoiled. Now that you know what channel the egg passes through in the chicken's body to get to your plate, you will realize why some eggs may have dried manure or dirt on them no matter how quickly you collect them out of the nest. The verdict on whether or not to wash eggs is highly debatable. This is because egg-shells are porous, and they have a micro membrane coating on them called a "bloom". The blooms purpose is to keep potential baby chicks and their environment safe and clean. Due to the natural bloom, bacteria have a hard time getting inside a dry eggshell. However, washing dirty eggs removes the bloom and allows bacteria inside the egg. Also, washing dirty eggs in cool water creates a "vacuum" effect that pulls unwanted bacteria inside the egg even faster. So, the best solution is prevention. In an attempt to prevent your eggs from being "dirty" in the first place, clean your nest boxes often. Obviously, this is not as easy if your chickens are nesting in areas other than the provided nest boxes. This is another reason to encourage them to lay in the designated areas. A constant supply of fresh shavings/bedding helps tremendously with keeping eggs clean once they're initially laid.

Secondly, place your roosting bars *higher* than your nesting boxes. Being a prey animal, chickens prefer to roost in the highest part of the coop as possible. If the only thing they have in their coop to sit on or in is their nesting boxes, they will do so, and they will soil the shavings meant to keep the eggs clean. Building their roosting areas higher than their nesting areas will discourage them from roosting in and soiling their boxes. While these tips will help prevent most of your eggs from getting dirty, it is almost impossible to prevent all of them. While you may choose to allow the dirty eggs to be hatched by your hen, or yourself, being dirty is not a reason to write them off for breakfast. Egg cleaning options include sandpaper-use a fine grit sandpaper to gently sand off any soiled areas of the egg. Even though this damages some of the bloom coating, it helps prevent the "vacuum" effect by keeping the egg dry.

If you do choose to use water to clean your eggs, do so with warm/hot water (that is approximately twenty degrees (or more) hotter than the egg itself). Ideally, only wash eggs that are visibly soiled. Anything that comes in that is visibly clean can go straight into the carton. (Winger, n.d.)

Eggs can be kept on the countertop. However, like with any food product, cool temperatures help reduce bacteria growth and extend shelf life so the refrigerator is also an option for storing your eggs, just as you would with grocery store eggs. Eggs that have potentially had some or all of their bloom removed through slight scrubbing or washing should definitely be kept in the refrigerator. You can even place eggs that you intend to incubate later in the refrigerator for up to two weeks with no reduced fertility side effects! Just be sure to place the eggs large end up in the carton.

Incubating Eggs and Hatching Chicks

Now that you're getting eggs on a regular basis, the question becomes do you want to eat them or incubate them (assuming you are not letting the hen hatch them herself)? If you decide you want to give incubating a try, you'll want to purchase an incubator. Depending on the size and goal of your operation, you can purchase a good incubator from $50 to upwards of ten times that amount! If you are just planning to incubate a few eggs to get the hang of it, a simple Styrofoam incubator may be a good starting point for you. While it's not a requirement, a chicken egg incubating pro would generally recommend that you buy an incubator with an auto-turner, which turns the eggs over periodically to prevent the embryo from sticking to the inside of the shell. Most incubators generally come with (or you can buy separately), a rack to hold the eggs. Depending on the type of incubator, they may offer racks that are sized for other eggs besides chickens. These may include quail, pheasant-chukar, turkey, or goose egg racks. Make sure the incubator you are purchasing has a rack(s) specifically for chicken eggs. If the hole is too small for a chicken egg, then the egg will not sit down properly in the rack and may fall off;, if the hole is too big, then the egg will fall through. Normally, the mother bird would turn the eggs several times a day with her feet once she starts sitting on them. This prevents the embryo from sticking to the inside of the shell, which can cause abnormal growth or even death.

Since you are essentially the mother bird in this scenario, the eggs need to either be turned by hand or incubated in an incubator with an automatic turner for the first 18 days of incubation (it takes 21 days incubation for a chicken egg to hatch). If you are turning the eggs by hand, use a non-toxic marker and mark the eggs with an "X" on one side and an "O" on the other, so when you are turning you can ensure that all eggs have been turned. Turn each egg at least three times daily. This can become tedious with a multitude of eggs, and it can be easy to forget. But, if you don't maintain a consistent rotation, it can result in the death of your growing embryos. This is why automatic egg turners are worth the extra expense! They are generally set to a default timer, which turns the egg every hour.

Also important to proper incubation is positioning of the eggs. Remember how we instructed to place the eggs large end up when storing in the carton? This is due to the air bubble inside an egg. A small air bubble forms in the large end of the egg under the shell soon after the egg is laid. There is a membrane separating the mass of the egg and the air bubble, which moves back and forth to relieve stress and pressure on the embryo resulting from changes in temperature. When an egg is just sitting on the ground or a flat surface, you can observe its normal position, with the large end slightly higher than the small pointed end. This is what tells us that the large end should be positioned upward when in the incubator. If the small end is consistently elevated instead, the embryo may become disoriented with its head toward the small end. This will most likely cause the chick to drown upon pipping (hatching).

Ventilation and humidity are the other two key factors that come into play while incubating chicken eggs. The drier the air is outside the egg, the quicker fluid inside the egg is depleted, and the faster the air bubble grows. Correct humidity inside the incubator prevents the air bubble from growing too big, which will deplete essential fluids. Correct humidity also helps prevent the egg from being too small, which would deny the chick enough air. Since there's no way to understand everything that's going on before the egg hatches, you will see the importance of correct humidity at the end of incubation. If you have achieved correct humidity throughout the incubation period, the air bubble will have enlarged to the point where the chick can reach its beak through the membrane wall, allowing it to breathe, before it pips through the shell. If the humidity has been too high, the chick may pip internally into the air bubble and drown in excess fluid. If humidity has been too low, the air bubble will be oversized and chick may be "shrink wrapped" in the inner membrane and unable to hatch (completely, if at all). In order to achieve this "perfect humidity" necessary for survival of your chicks, set the humidity at 45-50% for the first 18 days, then 65% for the last three days.

Equally important is the temperature of your incubator. As mentioned earlier, there are several incubator options, and the temperature will vary slightly depending on which type you purchase. A forced air incubator (with a fan) should have a temperature set at 99-99.5°F. A still air incubator should be slightly higher at101-102 °F. Depending on the type of incubator you purchase, you may need to place a thermometer and a hygrometer (a humidity measurer) inside your incubator. If you buy a higher scale incubator with a digital readout and regulator, you will just have to set it and check on it periodically to ensure that it is

working properly in terms of temperature, humidity, and

rotation of your eggs. Also, unless you buy a top of the line

incubator, you will most likely have to add water daily to

maintain the proper humidity. If you have a simpler

incubator, you can change the humidity by placing a tray of

water within the incubator. You can increase the humidity

by having a bigger surface area of water, and decrease the

humidity by having a smaller surface area of water.

Regardless of the type of incubator you purchase,

you should set it to the numbers and levels you want when

first bringing it home so that it can run for at least 24 hours

before you put your eggs in it. This will give the numbers

time to level out so that the conditions will be optimal

when you are ready to start incubating your eggs. Do not

try to block any holes that appear to be purposefully cut

into your incubator. Remember that eggs are porous, and

proper ventilation is important to prevent bacteria

growth/embryo suffocation. Imagine being in a hot, humid room all the time with no air flow-not ideal growing conditions right?

Once your incubator has been running properly for at least 24 hours, it's time to start incubating your eggs. You want to select clean, even-shaped, undamaged, and most importantly, fertile eggs for incubating. In nature, 100% fertility is rare, and your fertile rate will vary between 55% - 95% based on season, condition, and type of birds. Expect 50% - 75% of your fertile eggs to hatch when you first start learning about incubating. For this reason, it's recommended that you incubate more eggs than you want chicks. Unless you crack them open (which defeats the purpose), the fertility of eggs cannot be determined without incubating them. After 5-7 days in the incubator, white or light colored shelled eggs can be candled to see if embryos have developed. "Candling" involves taking a flashlight or candler (an apparatus made specifically for this task), and holding it on the egg in a dark room to see if there are signs of development. If you don't see any development by day 10, it is best to discard these "clear" eggs. This is because non-developing eggs may rot and explode within the incubator, which can cover the good eggs in unwanted bacteria and possibly prevent hatching (not to mention a foul smelling incubator). You can continue to candle the eggs throughout incubation to ensure that they are all developing at a similar rate, but be careful not to leave the incubator open for too long or the eggs may get too cold.

After some practice, you will be able to easily identify chicks which may have started to develop, but have died within the egg for one reason or another. Fertile eggs can be obtained easiest from online sellers, but "easiest" does not necessarily mean it's the best option. Eggs that have to be shipped are almost always sold with a "no guarantee" from the seller due to so many potential shipping complications that may hinder your eggs from hatching. Complications include delayed transportation times, loose or damaged air cells, or rough conditions that may cause the eggs to crack or break within the shipping box. This can be especially disappointing if you have spent a large amount of money for pure-bred hatching eggs. Ideally, try to obtain your fertile eggs from someone locally so you can pick them up yourself. Ask your local feed store if they have fertile eggs for sale or a local farmer recommendation. If you do decide to risk it and try shipped eggs, they should be allowed to "rest" for 24 hours prior to setting (in the incubator). This allows the contents of the eggs to settle. Place the shipped eggs upright, large end up, in an egg carton or something similar. We've already discussed the importance of placing the egg large end up.

Once you have chosen and incubated your fertile chicken eggs for 18 days, it is time to enter the phase known as "lockdown." Lockdown is the last 3 days of incubation, when humidity should be raised to 65% (to help the chick pip through the tough egg shell). If the humidity isn't rising the way you want, try placing a sponge within the water tray to help increase it. Try to avoid opening the incubator much within these last three days to avoid letting the necessary humidity out. Since your eggs should have all been placed in the incubator at the same time, they all should hatch within 24 hours of each other on Day 21. New chicks will appear wet and tired when they first hatch, but that's totally normal, they did put in some hard work getting out of their shell! Allow them to dry out and fluff up for 2-3 days in the incubator before removing them to the brooder. If incubated by the mother hen, normally she would not take them out of the nest until after this period anyways. The chicks do not need food and water during this time, as newly hatched chicks can survive for 2-3 days on their yolk which they absorb during the hatching process. Remember, this concept is what allows hatcheries to ship you newly hatched chicks without them dehydrating or starving while in shipment. (How to Incubate & Hatch Eggs - Just 21 Days From Egg to Chicken, 2013)

Parasites and Disease

You have now came full circle with your chickens. Whether you decided to start with eggs, chicks, adults, or do the whole cycle over again with incubation, hopefully you are better educated now than when you started. While you're well on your way to being a "pro" chicken keeper, something that you hopefully have not run into, but is always a possibility, are parasites and/or disease in your birds. While no chicken lover wishes for these problems, preventing and curing them quickly is especially important if you are raising your birds for meat or egg consumption. Many chicken keepers rally for vaccinating all birds against several common diseases, while many others argue that a well maintained flock will have little trouble with parasites or disease. Regardless of which opinion is yours, knowledge of potential trouble will hopefully help keep your run-ins with these problems short and quickly resolved. Common diseases in chickens include Avian/Fowl Pox, Botulism, Fowl Cholera, Infectious Bronchitis, Infectious Coryza, Mareks Disease, Moniliasis (Thrush), Mycoplasmosis/CRD/Air Sac Disease, Newcastle Disease, Omphalitis (Mushy Chick), and Pullorum.

Avian/Fowl Pox symptoms include white spots on the skin; combs that turn into scabby sores; white membranes and ulcers in mouth and or/on the trachea. All ages can be affected and in laying hens, laying will stop if the chicken is infected with Avian/Fowl Pox. This is a viral disease which can be transmitted by mosquitoes, other chickens with pox, and contaminated surfaces. Treatment includes supportive care such as warm dry quarters, and soft food. Many birds with good care can survive. There is a vaccine available for this disease if you should so choose.

Note that there is no known evidence that this is the same disease as "chicken pox" that affects humans, and as far as we know, it cannot be transferred from a chicken to a human.

Botulism symptoms include tremors that quickly progress to paralysis of the body, including breathing, which causes death within a few hours. With botulism, the feathers of the bird will pull out easily. Botulism is caused by a bacterial byproduct and by eating or drinking infected food or water. There is no vaccine available for this disease, but an antitoxin may be available from your veterinarian. Attempt to prevent spreading the bacteria by locating and removing the source, which is usually a decaying carcass or found in insects that fed on the meat or the water that the carcass may be in.

Fowl cholera is usually found in birds over four months of age. They will have greenish diarrhea, difficulty breathing, swollen joints, darkened head and wattles, and often a quick death. Fowl cholera is another bacterial disease often transmitted by wild birds, raccoons, possums, and rats. However, it can also be transmitted bird to bird and on contaminated soil, equipment, shoes, clothing or contaminated food or water. A vaccine is available but can only be administered by your state Department of Agriculture. There is no treatment available if your birds have already contracted this disease however. Unfortunately, all infected birds should be "put down" to prevent the spread of infection.

Respiratory birds can be highly detrimental to backyard flocks due to their ease of transmittal from bird to bird. Infection bronchitis can be diagnosed by observing coughing, sneezing, and/or watery discharge from the eyes and nose. Infected hens will stop laying. It is a viral disease that is highly contagious and spreads through the air, contact, and contaminated surfaces.

Infectious Coryza can be diagnosed by observing swollen heads, combs and wattles, eyes that are swollen shut, sticky discharge from the eyes and nose, and moist areas under the wings. It is a bacterial disease transmitted through carrier birds, contaminated surfaces, and drinking water. There is no available vaccine and infected birds should be "put down" as they will remain carriers for life.

Marek's Disease is a well-known viral disease in the chicken keeping community. It primarily affects chicks under 20 weeks of age. It causes external and internal tumors, the irises of the eye turns gray and don't react to light, and paralysis is the most obvious sign. Marek's Disease is very contagious and can be contracted by the chick inhaling shed skin cells or feather dust from other infected birds. There is no treatment available and it carries a high death rate. Any survivors will be carriers for life. It is best prevented by a vaccine which is given to day old chicks. If ordering from a hatchery, this is often one of the vaccine options that you can request be given when purchasing your chicks.

A fungal disease, Moniliasis, more commonly known as Thrush, can be contracted through moldy feed and water or surfaces contaminated by infected birds. Its symptoms are a white cheesy substance in the crop, ruffled feathers, droopy appearance, poor laying, white crusty or inflamed vent area, and increased appetite. There is no vaccine available for it but you can obtain Nystatin or another antifungal medication from a veterinarian. Also, watch out for it as it often occurs after antibiotic treatment has been given to birds for other, non-related reasons.

Mycoplasmosis/CRD/Air Sac Disease is carried by wild birds but also can be contracted through other birds and even through the egg to a chick from an infected hen. In mild form it causes weakness and poor laying. However, in its acute form it can cause breathing problems, coughing, sneezing, swollen and infected joints, and even death.

There is a vaccine available and antibiotics can be obtained from a veterinarian for already infected birds.

Newcastle disease is another well-known viral disease among chicken keepers. Its symptoms include wheezing, difficulty breathing, nasal discharge, cloudy eyes, laying stops, paralysis of legs, wings, and the most obvious signs are twisted heads and necks. It is highly contagious and contracted through infected chickens and wild birds, but can also be carried on shoes, clothes, and surfaces. There is a vaccine available but no treatment once a bird has it. While birds under six months usually die from the disease, older birds can recover and will not be carriers.

Omphalitis, also known as mushy chick, is a bacterial infection of the navel due to unclean surfaces or chicks with weak immune systems. It can also spread from chick to chick on contaminated surfaces. Infected newly hatched chicks will have enlarged, bluish, inflamed naval areas and may have a bad smell, or be drowsy or weak chicks. Antibiotics and clean housing sometimes helps, but most infected chicks will die. Healthy chicks should immediately be removed to clean quarters. **Gloves and caution should be taken when handling as staph and strep which cause this disease CAN infect humans.**

Pullorum is another (viral) disease that can infect chicks. The chicks will be inactive, have white diarrhea with pasted rear ends, and difficulty breathing, or they can die without symptoms. Older birds may have coughing, sneezing, or poor laying. It is contracted through carrier birds and contaminated surfaces, clothing, and shoes. Most infected chicks will die, and all of those that don't should be "put down" as even the ones which recover will be carriers. There is no vaccine, but there is a blood test to find carriers. (Common Chicken Illnesses and Treatments, n.d.) The U.S. is trying to eradicate this disease through its National Poultry Improvement Plan (NPIP).

The NPIP was "established in the early 1930's to provide a cooperative industry, state, and federal program through which new diagnostic technology can be effectively applied to the improvement of poultry and poultry products throughout the country." It was initiated to eliminate Pullorum Disease caused by Salmonella pullorum which was rampant in poultry and could cause upwards of 80% mortality in baby poultry in the early 1900s. It was later expanded to include testing and monitoring for Salmonella typhoid, Salmonella enteritidis, Mycoplasma gallisepticum, Mycoplasma synoviae, Mycoplasma meleagridis, and Avian Influenza. It also currently includes commercial poultry, turkeys, waterfowl, exhibition poultry, backyard poultry, and game birds. The blood test is a free test which can be scheduled through your state's Department of Agriculture office. If you chose earlier on to receive shipped, fertile eggs for incubating, the seller had to be NPIP certified (meaning his/her flock has passed the blood test) to ship eggs across state lines. NPIP certified means that not only have your birds been tested clean for Pullorum, but also that you only purchase new birds from other NPIP certified flocks. It is a great program to look into once you become a more established chicken keeper and especially if you intend to ship eggs/birds in the future. (Poultry Disease Information, n.d.)

When raising chickens, more often seen than full fledge poultry diseases are internal and external parasites. One of the most common parasitic roundworms occurring in chickens are Ascarids, or large intestinal roundworms. They are known as this because adult worms are one and half to three inches long, which can easily be seen with the naked eye and is large compared to a chicken's body. Chickens that are heavily infected with these worms may appear droopy, emaciated, and have diarrhea. The worms cause reduced efficiency of feed utilization and even death. Birds become infected by eating roundworm eggs that have reached the infective stage. Roundworm females lay thick heavy shelled eggs in the intestine of the bird that passes in the feces. A small embryo develops in the egg but doesn't hatch for two to three weeks; this is the infective stage. The embryonated egg is very hardy though and it may live for a whole year before hatching! This factor combined with the fact that disinfectants and other cleaning agents don't kill eggs under farm conditions make this a parasite's life cycle hard to eradicate. The treatment of choice for the adult roundworm is piperazine, however, it removes ONLY the adult worm. This parasite can be controlled by strict sanitation. This means if birds are confined, clean the area thoroughly before a new group is brought in. Segregate birds by age groups, and as always, because young birds systems are more fragile, use particular care with the sanitation of young birds housing. If birds are free ranged, use a clean (new) range for each new group of birds.

Tapeworms, also known as cestodes, are flattened,

ribbon shaped worms made up of numerous segments or divisions. Tapeworms are a common infection when raising chickens. The divisions break off from the main part of the worm and resemble grains of rice. The tapeworms spend part of their lives in intermediate hosts. Your chicken becomes infected by eating the intermediate hosts which can include snails, slugs, beetles, ants, grasshoppers, earthworms, and houseflies, etc. The intermediate host itself became infected by eating the eggs of tapeworms that are passed in the bird feces, a seemingly never-ending cycle of repeat infection. These worm infestations are most easily controlled by preventing the birds from eating the infected intermediate host. This is easier said than done if you plan on regularly free ranging your bird. The infections can also be controlled by regular treatment with the drugs fenbendazole or leviamisole.

A similarly sounding name but completely different parasite is the gapeworm, also known as Syngamus trachea.

These are a round red worm that attach to the trachea or windpipe of a bird and cause the disease referred to as "gapes". This term describes the open-mouth breathing that is done by infected birds. The worms can easily block the trachea, and so heavily infected birds may die from suffocation. Besides being known as the "red worm," the gapeworm is also known as "forked-worm" because the male and female are joined in permanent copulation appearing like the letter "Y". Both sexes of the worm attach to the lining of the trachea with their windparts. Fenbendazole is again the ideal drug of choice for prevention. However, it should be noted that it is not presently approved for use in birds by the Food and Drug Administration.

Some parasites presence have no marked symptoms or pathology that can be blamed on it, but rather are a vector of other agents. Such is the case with cecal worms, also know as Heterakis gallinae. This is the agent that causes "blackhead," a poultry disease which affects the liver and cecum. It is a protozoan parasite that is carried in the cecal worm egg and is transmitted from bird to bird through this egg. Again, the cecal worm is a parasite that can be effectively treated with fenbendazole.

External parasites can be equally prolific on chickens as internal parasites. The most common include poultry mites and poultry lice. Unfortunately, mites come in quite a variety. Some are blood-suckers, some burrow into the skin or live on or in the feathers, but others cross back into the internal category and can occur in the air passages, lungs, liver and other internal organs. They can cause retarded growth, reduced egg production, lowered vitality, damaged plumage, and even death. Unlike worms seen moving in the feces, they will not be as easily visible without careful examination. The worst offender seems to be the Northern Fowl Mite or Ornithonyssus sylviarum, which is a frequent and serious pest of chickens that remains on the bird and does more damage than any other species of mite. Other types with tell-tale names include the scaly-leg mite (Knemidocoptes mutans) and the Depluming Mite (Knemidocoptes laevis). Regular inspection of your birds, coops, and a spraying program of both the birds and premises is the most effective treatment for all mite species. Spray the birds and facilities with the appropriate solution of permethrin, and repeat every month or two.

Poultry lice's primary affects, though less directly damaging than mites, are the irritations they cause the bird. This leads the bird to become restless, not feed, and not sleep well. Injuries may occur due to pecking or scratching at themselves, and body weight and egg production may droop. While the same measures used to eliminate mite populations should be used for controlling and treating lice, it is more important to apply the insecticides directly to the bird's body rather than the premises. This is because lice will remain alive while on feathered hosts, but will soon die if removed. Whereas with mites, they will leave and return to the host several times throughout their life cycle. (Diseases of Poultry, n.d.)

Conclusion

Now you have everything you need to get started raising chickens, from buying chicks or adults, raising chicks or adults, housing, feeding, and what to do if they become ill. You are well on your way to becoming a bonafide chicken keeper. Finally, if you enjoyed this book, I would be so grateful if you would leave a review for this book on Amazon. This helps me share the good news of raising chickens with more people like you! You can simply click HERE to leave a review. Thank you! Good luck and happy peeping!

Work Cited

Backyard Chicken Farmer. (n.d.). *Backyard Chickens-The 5 Best Breeds for Egg Layers*. Retrieved from Backyard Chicken Farmer: http://thebackyardchickenfarmer.com/backyard-chickens-5-best-egg-layers/

Chicken Help Q: Is it possible for several roosters to coexist peacefully together in our flock? (n.d.). Retrieved from myPetChicken: http://www.mypetchicken.com/backyard-chickens/chicken-help/Is-it-possible-for-several-roosters-to-coexist-H154.aspx

Combs. (n.d.). Retrieved from University of Illinois Extension Incubation and Embryology: https://extension.illinois.edu/eggs/res11-combs.html

Common Chicken Illnesses and Treatments. (n.d.). Retrieved from For Dummies: http://www.dummies.com/how-to/content/common-chicken-illnesses-and-treatments.seriesId-137004.html

Damerow, G. (2012, June/July). The Chicken Encyclopedia. In G. Damerow, *The Chicken Encyclopedia* (p. 235).

Diseases of Poultry. (n.d.). Retrieved from Mississippi State University Extension: http://extension.msstate.edu/agriculture/livestock/poultry/diseases-poultry

Foley, D. (2015, May 21). *Everything You Need To Know About Raising Backyard Chickens*. Retrieved from Rodale's OrganicLife: http://www.rodalesorganiclife.com/garden/everything-you-need-know-about-raising-backyard-chickens

Food and Agriculuture Organization of the United States Statistics Division. (2013). *Production/Live Animals*.

Retrieved from FAOSTAT:
http://faostat3.fao.org/browse/Q/QA/E

For Dummies. (n.d.). *How to Determine Your Flock Size and Space Requirements*. Retrieved from Gardening with Free-Range Chickens for Dummies: http://www.dummies.com/how-to/content/how-to-determine-your-flock-size-and-space-require.html

Gautheir, J., & Ludlow, R. (n.d.). *The Digestive System of A Chicken*. Retrieved from Chicken Health for Dummies: http://www.dummies.com/home-garden/hobby-farming/raising-chickens/the-digestive-system-of-a-chicken/

Hackle. (n.d.). Retrieved from Merriam-Webster: http://www.merriam-webster.com/dictionary/hackle

How to Incubate & Hatch Eggs - Just 21 Days From Egg to Chicken. (2013, 07 31). Retrieved from BackYard Chickens: http://www.backyardchickens.com/a/how-to-incubate-hatch-eggs-just-21-days-from-egg-to-chicken

Jeffrey A. Coutts, G. C. (2007). Optimum Egg Quality A Practical Approach. In G. C. Jeffrey A. Coutts, *Optimum Egg Quality A Practical Approach*. The State of Queensland, Australia (through its Department of Primary Industries and Fisheries) and DSM Nutritional Products Ltd., 2007.

Merriam-Webster. (n.d.). *Merriam-Webster*. Retrieved from Merriam-Webster: http://www.merriam-webster.com/dictionary/cockerel

Mormino, K. S. (n.d.). *Feeding Chickens at Different Ages*. Retrieved from The Chicken Chick: http://www.the-chicken-chick.com/2012/11/feeding-chickens-at-different-ages.html

Morning Chores. (n.d.). *11 Best Chicken Breeds for Meat (and Dual Purpose) to Raise in Your Backyard.* Retrieved from Morning Chores: http://morningchores.com/meat-chickens/

Murray McMurray Hatchery. (n.d.). *Chick Care Tips.* Retrieved from Murray McMurray Hatchery: https://www.mcmurrayhatchery.com/chickcare.html

Poultry Disease Information. (n.d.). Retrieved from The National Poultry Improvement Plan: http://www.poultryimprovement.org/default.cfm;jsessio nid=AE0E997539E567334696CC375D80F8C8.cfusion? CFID=8314838&CFTOKEN=474394fd317848bc-3312B170-D936-BFCE-33BCFFB578F9111D

Stromberg's Chicks & Game Birds Unlimited. (n.d.). *Ornamental Chickens.* Retrieved from Stromberg's Chicks & Game Birds Unlimited: Stromberg's Chicks & Game Birds Unlimited

The 9 Comb Types. (2015, 06 13). Retrieved from Backyard Chickens: http://www.backyardchickens.com/a/the-9-comb-types

The Livestock Conservancy. (n.d.). *Heritage Chicken.* Retrieved from The Livestock Conservancy: https://livestockconservancy.org/index.php/heritage/inter nal/heritage-chicken

The My Pet Chicken Guide to Chicken Care. (n.d.). Retrieved from my Pet Chicken: http://www.mypetchicken.com/backyard-chickens/chicken-care/chapter-4-caring-for-baby-chicks.aspx?t=1

Wattle. (n.d.). Retrieved from Merriam-Webster: http://www.merriam-webster.com/dictionary/wattle

Winger, J. (n.d.). *Eggs: To Wash or Not to Wash?* Retrieved from The Prairie Homestead: http://www.theprairiehomestead.com/2011/10/eggs-to-wash-or-not-to-wash.html

Printed in Great Britain
by Amazon